The
ABCs
of Praying for Students

The Most Important Tool Not On Your
School Supply List

by Julie Sanders

ISBN: 978-1-7332559-0-5

Cover art and design by Christen Price Studio, www.christenprice.com
Printing by Dothan Printing
Edited by Samantha Whittington

First printing, July 2019
Printed in the United States of America

Christen Price Studio
P.O. Box 25
Pinckard, AL 36371

www.christenprice.com

This book is dedicated to my own two students, JoHanna and Jacob, who taught me my greatest lessons and now have students of their own.

TABLE OF CONTENTS

ABCs of Prayer

Foreword

Sitting in a cabin just outside Winter Park, Colorado, I couldn't believe that I had arrived. I'd just flown halfway across the country for a weekend retreat with a group of women that I'd never met in person, and only vaguely knew from their online presence. Around twenty-five women booked airplane tickets for this weekend to spend time together as a group of moms so we could dream, plan, and pray for our futures and how the Lord would use us as a collective group.

Arriving with a few others, I noticed that I was one of the younger women in the group. Some of them had already developed friendships from years of working together in ministry, and I immediately felt fear swirl around inside my stomach as I introduced myself, found my room, and began to make small talk with the others. The first night that we gathered together, we made a spaghetti dinner, and all sat in a long row of farmhouse tables so we could get to know one another better. Sitting within talking distance, was Julie Sanders. With her dark hair, generous smile, and calming personality, she immediately made me feel comfortable and welcome.

Julie shared her background with me that evening, how she and her husband worked cross-culturally, and their children grew up both in the States and in Asia. During her years serving overseas and while she was home, Julie taught school and equipped mothers with resources on parenting. She showed these families the love of Jesus through language, science, and math. Julie was also a photographer and had a display of images that told what life was like for families in these underdeveloped countries. She did not boast about her life's work but drew me in story by story.

At the time of our first meeting, my twin girls were two and Julie and her family lived in Tennessee. Even though I met many women that weekend, Julie was someone who I kept turning to in conversation. Maybe it was our shared interest in sweet tea and SEC sports, but I think she drew me in because of the way she spoke about life. She had two children that were nearing the end of high school, so I asked her lots of questions about motherhood, parenting, and raising children to love the Lord. Julie was

1

patient with my questions and responded each time in a calm and caring manner. Julie gave me confidence that weekend as a young mother, and I believe that through this devotional, she will provide you with confidence as a mother too.

The ABCs of Praying for Students began through Julie's love of teaching. What started as a simple bookmark tool for prayer, is now available as a twenty-six-day devotional that will guide your heart with prayers as your student matures in school each year. Julie and I both believe that when a parent understands how to apply prayer to academic settings, we are empowered as mothers to do the work as our child's divine advocate. We know that preparing your child to go back to school is busy—picking out school supplies, meeting their teachers, signing your children up for co-curricular activities—and it's easy to feel overwhelmed by all the things to do for your kids. Not to mention all the jitters that everyone has before school begins when it comes to what friends will be in their class, what activities they will get picked for, and how they will get along with their teachers!

Allow Julie's words to be a breath of peace to your parent soul this school year. Each day, she will guide you through praying for your student's attitude, character, and knowledge with a key Bible verse, short devotional, and at the end Julie offers you ways to dig deeper and to have conversations with your child through table talk. Our prayer is for this devotional to not only provide you a way to pray for your student, but that you will also deepen your relationship with the Lord as your student begins a new school year. We hope that you enjoy this devotional, and it is something that you can turn to each year as your student grows.

Celebrating you,

Christen

Introduction

I wasn't born into a praying family. I was born into a working family. My mom went to a one room schoolhouse and gave up her acceptance to nursing school when there was no money in her Appalachian family of nine. Neither of my parents went to college. Both my mom and dad were determined to give us more than they had. Thankfully, before I started kindergarten, my parents asked desperate questions about how to get real success. That need to know led to a new everything in our lives, including school. My learning journey changed when I became a student supported by the prayers of my parents.

My heart is full knowing you picked up this book out of a desire to see your student succeed. You're that adult who wants to lift a child in learning and in life. You do so much, because you care so much. But what if I told you the most significant supply for your student's success will be left off the back-to-school list? We can't stock up on this education essential, though I know you would if you could. What our learners need more than anything is our prayers, prayers fueled by your genuine love and a heart full of hope for the student on your mind.

The ABCs of Praying for Students began as a bookmark for grown ups who support kids of all ages in their learning journey. That includes parents, but also teachers, grandparents, mentors, foster parents, and friends. Character qualities and truths apply to learners in their earliest years to students launching into life. The alphabet provides the framework for the most important objectives to master along the way.

In each devotional, you'll find five elements to shape the way you support your student.
1. A letter of the alphabet connected to a character objective
2. A Bible verse to help us learn what God says
3. A devotional with practical insights applying truth to life and learning
4. A few tips to help you take an action step of response
5. Ideas for Table Talk to extend the devotion in conversation with your student

Sometimes, there are things to know before taking a class or using a tool.

While any caring grown up can pick up *The ABCs of Praying for Students* and find insights for student success, there is a "prerequisite" to know. From my experiences as a mom, teacher, professor, tutor, mentor, and education leader, you should know I believe prayer is what students need more than all the supplies grown ups sacrifice and search for.

In these 26 devotions, I've included verses from the Bible, illustrations to explain them, and ideas for how to apply them, because I'm sure God has a plan for every student cared for by every reader of this book. God's Word tells us He is the Maker of each child, and He knows each one—gifts they have, passions they find, challenges they face, failures they'll endure, and successes they'll achieve. No degree of giftedness or intelligence can bring a student real peace without knowing Him. As you allow *The ABCs of Praying for Students* to motivate, inform, and fill your personal prayers for the learners you love, their learning journey will change.

More than academic achievement, each student needs to learn that sin is our greatest disability. It keeps us from the relationship with God we're meant to have. He provides answers for us. As you read these 26 devotions, each character quality is the result of God's plan at work in the life of your student. In the stories and examples, you will hear me share how God uses hard lessons to lead us to life. Each of *The ABCs of Praying for Students* is shaped with these beliefs.

To make the most of time in *The ABCs,* I encourage you to do one or more of these:
- On each page, make notes of specific applications to your student.
- Choose one action step that works best for you and do it right away.
- Use Table Talk the same day you read the devotion.
- Don't let the absence of a "table" stop you—those conversations are great anywhere.
- Ask a friend to read and pray with you, so you can learn, share, and pray together.

I'm praying *The ABCs of Praying for Students* will help launch your learner on God's path for them. Whether you school in a traditional classroom, a co-op, homeschool, or a one room schoolhouse like my mom, God wants to use the experience of education to teach your child the truths that matter most. The prayers of a caring adult are the greatest source of power leading to lasting student success in learning and life.

Thank you for praying. It's going to change a life.

ATTITUDE

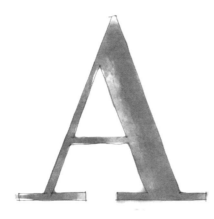

"Let the words of my mouth and the meditation of my heart be acceptable in your sight, O Lord, my rock and my redeemer."

Psalm 19:14

Check out supply lists posted at your local store or on your school's website, but you won't find it. Scan your teacher's wish boards in hallways, but it's not there. Scan the descriptions and syllabi of what students will learn and outcomes they'll achieve, but you won't find it included. Bumped out by boxes of tissues, gluesticks, and crayons—and overshadowed by vocabulary and math skills, a good attitude is the essential supply and the success every child needs.

Before school even begins and at the start of each new learning day, moms tend to tuck reminders into the ears, and sometimes the lunch boxes, of their learner. "Pay attention. Do what the teacher says. Write down your homework. Bring home your backpack." Mom-talk lodges in the ears and minds of our kiddos from prek to college, as we influence their actions. It's a relief to see them do right, isn't it? And it doesn't hurt our cred as a mom, either. But we can pray for more than good actions. We can pray for the growth of a good attitude.

Attitude takes longer to learn than actions, but attitude lasts longer than actions. We often pray short-term and short-sighted prayers about what presses in at the moment. Bullies on the playground, loneliness at lunch, and understanding in math. But what if we go to God about what matters more in the bigger picture of learning, deep learning?

Oh God, would you plant deep seeds of joy in my child's character? Would you create patterns of perseverance and etch out traits of thankfulness? I'm willing to wait for these greater lessons, Lord, if you will sow these attitudes into the heart of my child.

Actions change with developmental stages, but attitudes have a way of persisting in layers as children grow.

"The good person out of the good treasure of his heart produces good, and the evil person out of his evil treasure produces evil, for out of the abundance of the heart his mouth speaks." (Luke 6:45)

More than complying with rules and expectations of parents and teachers, what we really want is for children to grow up into caring about pleasing their Heavenly Father. Actions and words expose the attitude of the growing heart. This is a bigger ask when we go to pray for our kids, but it's the ask we want.

"Let the words of my mouth and the meditation of my heart be acceptable in your sight, O Lord." I want the thoughts, motivations, and hopes of my heart and mind to please God. I want the thoughts, motivations, and hopes of my child's heart and mind to please God. I'm praying for more than just compliant actions.

Classrooms have a way of arousing attitudes. There are other adults to obey, a variety of peers with diverse backgrounds, differing beliefs (even among people of like faith), personal performance challenges, and the unpredictable concoction of mixing it all together. It's enough to press in on the attitude or a child or a grown up. Will it result in anger? Resentment? Pride? Paranoia? Self-loathing? Insecurity?

Attitude takes longer to learn than actions, but attitude lasts longer than actions. Hold out in prayer for attitudes acceptable in God's sight.

Digging Deeper

4 Ways to Hold Out for Acceptable Attitudes:

- Tell your child what attitude you expect or hope for. Be descriptive.
- Model the attitude you want to see grow in your child.
- Hold out for God's pleasure over your own.
- Find out what kind of thinking pleases God. Check out Philippians 4:8.

Table Talk

- Do you know someone at school who has a good attitude? How can you tell?
- Are there times when it's hard to have a good attitude? What makes it hard?
- I want you to know I'm praying for you to have an attitude that pleases God, and that will be an attitude that pleases me.

6

BOLDNESS

"The Lord is my light and my salvation; whom shall I fear? The Lord is the stronghold of my life; of whom shall I be afraid?"

Psalm 27:1

We sat cross-legged in a circle, connected by the bonds between students and teacher. Show-and-tell brought out a favorite rock, a family photo, a team jersey. Treasures entrusted to the circle. But his hands were empty the day he asked if he could share what he witnessed over the weekend. "Of course," I invited, as he announced, "I went to a baptism. Does anyone know what a baptism is?" Met by puzzled faces, he asked if he could explain what it is. I knew it was a big moment.

Since a child took the initiative, I nodded and sat back. He took a deep breath and leaned forward. A clear explanation rolled out of how being put down in water and raised back up is a picture of how God takes an old life, cleans it, and brings it to new life. "He does this," the little preacher said, "through His own Son Jesus who died to pay for what people owe for their wrong-doing." The young theologian shared God's plan for mankind in a clear, child-like way with his friends who had never seen such a thing.

Big things will happen in a child's life, and they need to be bold.

Every child will face a big moment. It may be a moment when truth should be told. It may be a moment when justice should be done. It may be a moment when the weak should be defended. A big moment is sure to come, "whom shall I fear?"

It takes boldness to stand for what's good if it means standing alone. Every mom would gladly stand behind her child staring down the haters or the scoffers. But in most bold moments, mom won't be there. That's part of what makes it bold. And for those children and young people who get to experience the exhilaration of God being the stronghold of their life to answer their fear, they grow up with a valuable understanding. Even when their parents aren't there, they'll be okay. They're raised to be interdependent with loved ones in their life, but they are able to function independently in the strength God gives to fuel their boldness in big moments.

It's not easy for a child to learn the bold balance of overcoming fear without radiating aggression. When they're asked to speak up for truth or show up for the weak, their character has to step up and be personally bold in an honorable way. When we start to move away from home and family, it's easy for a child's "inner chicken" to take over. I remember as a first grader desperately wanting to tell my curly-haired friend that Jesus loves her, but I was afraid. Afraid of the teacher. Afraid of the principal. Afraid of other kids. Afraid of rejection. During indoor recess, I got up the nerve to meet my pal in the coat closet for a rapid-telling of how God so loved the world He gave His only Son. I hid behind sweatshirts and backpacks, when God wanted to empower me to bring my faith into the open. There will be big moments that call for boldness, but there will be a lot more small, unseen moments that call for kids to learn what it means to let their Light and Salvation be their Stronghold.

Our kids will have countless opportunities to practice boldness of spirit. School is a daily exercise in expressing who we are and what we believe. By the time I graduated from high school, the Lord brought me out of the coat closet and onto the graduation platform to pray in His name before my class of more than 600 peers. Big things will happen, and our kids need to be bold.

May God give our students strength within to be bold without.

Digging Deeper

4 Ways to Pray for your Student to Be Bold:

- Pray for bold friends to stand with your child in bold ways.
- Pray for adults to invite, allow, and encourage your child in bold moments.
- Pray for students around your child to be bold when they need an advocate.
- Pray for God to actively bless your child when they take a bold step.

Table Talk

- Can you think of a time you felt afraid, but you needed to speak up or take action? What did you do?
- Have you seen another student do something you think was bold?
- When you have a time you need to bold, I may not be there, but God will be.

COURAGE

"The true light, which gives light to everyone, was coming into the world."

John 1:9

Let's be honest. We don't want to pray for kid-courage, because we don't want our children to need to be courageous. But they will. Kids will need courage in classrooms and they will need courage for life.

Down the hallway, two lines of head to head first graders competed for math problems. Speed assured success, while not being fast guaranteed failure. From her end of line hiding place, Misty's face showed fear. Wringing hands gave away her worry. Oh, illusive courage.

My supervising teacher believed public pressure to perform produced better math. I saw only fear on Misty's face, her eyes searching for rescue or reassurance. If only courage could give voice to answers she knew when the room was quiet and we worked one on one. As a new teacher, I could only let her eyes meet mine to silently smile and speak comfort in her crisis.

Learning shouldn't include humiliating. Still, there will be times when students face unfair formats or undeserved defeats. Sometimes hardship can't be helped. We are tempted to extract them or confront the decision-maker, and sometimes we do, but sometimes students stay and battle. Kids need courage in classrooms.

When students step into an environment of peers and new grown ups, they will face moments when they must be brave. "Scary" feels different at each developmental level and for each unique child. For some, speed is the enemy. For others, attention stirs anxiety. Each child encounters their own challenge when courage is needed to face their "hard" in the world.

When God's Son Jesus came into the world, He brought light. Wherever His children take His light, they bring kindness and inspire courage both large and small. It's how a friend stands up against a bully. It's how a new student walks into a lunchroom. It's how a child faces the gauntlet of a math competition. It's how a student says the right thing in the face of wrong. It's how a teacher covers students when danger threatens. And after hard things, true light creates the courageous resilience kids need if they're going to grow up and engage the world.

Courage for the large and for the small never feels small. In classrooms or in life.

Sometimes the world will be hard, even hateful. It's not what we would choose for our children, but it's a challenge they will encounter. The true light of God's Son "gives light to everyone." Before a child has a personal relationship with Jesus, dark moments may help lead them to Him. Once a child knows Jesus personally, His light shines through them. As children grow up, what if they could be so courageous they inspire courage in others?

Parents, we could ask God to remove ridicule, pressure, bullies, defeats, threats, and hardships. But how much better if we pray that while they're in their classrooms, God would grow such great courage in our kids that it inspires courage in others?

I'm not sure what happened to Misty after first grade, but I'm sure hallway math was not the last gauntlet she faced. I pray our kid-courage coaching served her well beyond the classroom and in more than counting.

Digging Deeper

3 Stories to Tell

- Tell a story about a time you were afraid as a child.
- Tell a story about "resilience" and what it means to "come back" after being afraid or defeated.
- Tell a story about someone you know who acted in a courageous way.

Table Talk

- Put a candle on the table to observe. Talk about what light does in darkness.
- When darkness wants to snuff out light by making us afraid, how does God's Son Jesus help us have courage to shine?
- What's a "hard time" when you might need to be courageous? Imagine it and how you might act.
- How could we shine our light and help a friend who needs courage?

DISCERNMENT

"And it is my prayer that your love may abound more and more, with knowledge and all discernment, so that you may approve what is excellent, and so be pure and blameless for the day of Christ."

Philippians 1:9-10

I don't want kids who just follow rules. I want kids who follow wise patterns. We think of this as "discipline," choosing to follow what's good, based on what has been given or taught. This takes discernment, which some describe as wise decision-making. If discipline is consistently following wise patterns, discernment is figuring out what patterns are wise.

Discernment is cultivated from what children learn, equipping them in how to think. Armed with this asset for living well, discipline equips them in how to act. When our kiddos blend what they know with the wisdom to apply what they know, they can make "excellent" decisions and behave in a way that is abundantly loving to others.

It was indoor recess in kindergarten, with plenty of time for experimenting in reading the cues of my classmates. Watching two friends laughing together, I decided they must be friendly and safe. I had no sooner punctuated the end of my joke with a smile, than the larger of the two boys turned down towards my face and delivered the full force of his fist into my unprepared gut, sucking the wind out of my innocence. Misreading his cues, my childish assessment of who to trust was way off. Lesson learned. Not everyone who has a friend makes a good friend.

Children haven't ventured far into the early years when they are pressed to make a decision. Who will they choose for a friend? What version will they believe is true? When will they work and when will they play? Whose voice will they obey? Many moments of decision will be quick, as they learn how wisdom rewards and foolishness feels. Childhood is constructed from the building blocks of choices a child makes.

Most choices are small, taking place on stages with names like "playground" or "cafeteria" or "bedroom" or "classroom" or "website." Discernment to figure out how to live out what's been learned comes from a childhood of little decisions producing big direction for life.

Today's child has access to more information than ever. Students log in and out from under the watchful wisdom of parents or, sometimes, any adult. The World Wide Web may entangle children through their own exploration or the experience of classmates. Parents cannot monitor every opportunity for exposure, but we can carefully and prayerfully make decisions about technology. For many children in a technological age, there's too much information, but not enough discernment.

As children move into puberty to teenage years to young adulthood, decisions start to happen with more warning. Anticipating change and sorting through options calls for kids to use what they've been taught to translate into what they choose. Relationships. Careers. Education. Church life. Family. Students will carefully consider and discern what path to take, to "approve what is excellent." There will not be a list of rules to move through the journey to being grown up. Children need knowledge and discernment to know how to think and how to act.

Childhood is constructed from the building blocks of choices a child makes. Let's ask God to build our little ones into strong students for lifelong learning!

Digging Deeper

3 Questions to Ask

Read a favorite Bible verse out loud and ask a question to practice using knowledge for decision-making. (Ex. 1 John 1:9, Psalm 56:3)
- How would knowing this help you make an excellent decision?
- How could it look with your friends?
- What would it sound like (in your head) if you were thinking and deciding what to do?

Table Talk

- Tell about when you had a hard decision to make, but you remembered a Bible verse that helped you act in a right way.
- Ask each one to share about a choice they had to make today, big or small. How did they decide what to do?
- When we love each other, we take what we know and make the best decisions we can. Fill in the blank: I feel lots of love when you _____.

ENTHUSIASM

"Whatever you do, work heartily, as for the Lord and not for men."

Colossians 3:23

They hobbled in giggling, shuffling how they imagined grandmas and grandpas shuffle. Some grasped canes from home, where they drew on wrinkles with eyeliner and squeezed their eyes while powdering their hair. A few wide neckties and calico aprons rounded out their accessories. Shouts of "Happy 100th Day!" released them from the charade as they danced the dance of childhood. They tried to remember to bend over like they practiced before dissolving into laughter. No one has to teach a child enthusiasm.

But somewhere between cradle and classroom, some students have their God-given enthusiasm crushed. Innocent and imaginative, eager to please and participate, childish excitement may be stifled or starved. Circumstances can convince a child it's safer to hold back or hide, and enthusiasm may be the casualty.

Colossians speaks to the loss of the enthusiastic spirit God created within us. Life has a way of turning our attention to the things of earth and judgments of people around us. But the writer Paul encourages readers to "Set your minds on things that are above," (3:2a) and talks about living abundantly and with fullness. When we learn to think about the heavenly audience, we don't hold back from acting abundantly. Enthusiastically.

If we know Jesus Christ is Lord over everything on the earth where we do life with our children, and everything in heavenly places too, we can point our passions towards heavenly, lasting things. Wired to participate and please whole-heartedly, if Jesus is Lord of all of it, all of it is for Jesus.

It may be on the 1st day or the 100th day or Graduation Day, but our children will run into walls of judgment, mockery, exclusion, unkindness, and even rejection. Our hearts will hurt for them and their child-like enthusiasm that will take a beating. Home is the place where we strengthen their confidence in what matters most and who matters most. What's the focus of what we do? Who do we do it for? And because of that, how should we do it?

Whatever we do, let's do it with enthusiasm to please Jesus in heaven, not just people on earth. Parents have the opportunity to model this in front of and side by side their children. We don't get it right every time, but we keep aiming to please the one who is Lord over all we do. How we feed our family. How we keep a home. How we do marriage. How we do church. How we do our work. How we rest and play. Jesus is Lord over all of it, so we do all of it with gusto and eagerness.

Maybe you know what it is to have the wind sucked out of your enthusiasm. You may be a casualty of judgment, mockery, exclusion, unkindness, or rejection. Does enthusiastic freedom seem like a distant memory from your childhood days of long ago? As a parent, you may need healing to restore your own ability to act with an unhindered, heavenward spirit of abundance. It's worth pursuing, so we can be the all-in, enthusiastic parent our child needs as our Heavenly Father plans. Ask God to help you recapture it as you focus on doing whatever you do to bring Him joy. And as you do, ask Him to protect your child's enthusiasm from the crushers they'll encounter.

God has already produced enthusiasm in your child; now ask Him to protect it.

Digging Deeper

3 Questions to Ask and 3 Answers to Repeat

- What's the focus of what we do? What's important is what Jesus thinks.
- Who do we do it for? Jesus is the one whose opinion matters most.
- How should we do it? Jesus wants us to do what we do with a sincere heart.

Table Talk

- What do you get excited about at school?
- What is your least favorite job to do at home?
- Have you ever felt unsure about something you agreed to do? What happened?

FRIENDLINESS

"A man of many companions may come to ruin, but there is a friend who sticks closer than a brother."

Proverbs 18:24

She trembled the day she came to fourth grade. Others wouldn't understand the courage it took just to come, after losing familiar things that give a girl confidence to laugh and be silly. But this was a new start, and her mom said she would be safe. Hearing how terrifying it was to begin, the wise teacher gathered a small group of girls for lunch in her room, so the new girl could get acquainted quietly. Carried by her mom's prayers and her teacher's plans, she entered into making friends.

More than solving math problems, reading aloud, or presenting projects, making friends can be the most daunting challenge a student faces. Parents pray fervent prayers with images of crowded lunchrooms, sports team selections, or birthday party invitations in mind. Oh that our children would be spared isolation and gifted with friendship.

From their first days with peers, children look for others to know them, someone to be safe with. By establishing a connection with another child, they develop a sense of belonging and a source of support. Children look for someone who will cling to them despite the unpredictable, sometimes embarrassing, experiments of childhood. Such connection gives confidence to grow and develop as an individual.

As they grow older and more aware of peer opinions and influence, children look for friends who provide reliable relationships through changes they experience. It doesn't take a crowd. It only takes one.

We can't make friends for our children. It's one of their first steps towards independence, the choosing and cultivating of a friendship. But parents can create the space and the structure for good friendships, and we can pray.

Just as the wise teacher set aside a quiet place for a small group to get

16

acquainted with a frightened little girl, grown ups can influence opportunities for friendships to be born. It's a beautiful thing when a parent can work with a teacher as a partner for the friendships of their child. If a grown up wants to help give a child the gift of friendship, simple steps can be taken to create the environment for friendship to grow.

- Show what friendship looks like with your friends and your friendliness.
- Set aside space and time where a child can successfully navigate new people.
- Select a variety of peers to bring together to explore making connections.
- Support the first moments of awkwardness, but know how to step away.
- Say a prayer and trust God to grow your child through friend-making.

Crowded cafeterias and new classrooms can be daunting, but they provide places where students learn to exercise friendliness, make connections, and build community with those reliable ones they call "friend".

Digging Deeper

3 Ways to Pray

- Lord, please give my child a friend who will stick close as they grow up.
- Lord, would you help my child have a heart that wants to be a good friend?
- Lord, I'm asking you to give my child wisdom to know who is a good friend.

Table Talk

- Who do you think is a friend of yours who will stick by you?
- How does someone act if they want to make a friend?
- What would you sound like if you were trying to be a good friend?

GENEROSITY

"Each one must give as he has decided in his heart, not reluctantly or under compulsion, for God loves a cheerful giver."

2 Corinthians 9:7

When a parent really wants to be the room mom at school, the teacher waffles between wondering if there's a reason to be cautious or just grateful. Great room moms have one thing in common that we all hope our children will learn: generosity.

When Masie burst in with a toddler dangling on her finger, an infant strapped to her chest, and her student hiding behind her, she overflowed with eager offers to do whatever was needed in our classroom. It was the beginning of countless creative, messy, colorful, and joy-filled contributions to our first grade family. She never came with just enough or just because; she came with plenty out of a generous heart. And the children watched and learned.

Until then, toddler years were sprinkled with reminders to "share," but then they enter school and well-meaning moms create confusion. We label. Everything. The backpack, the schoolbox, the lunchbox, the tissues, the eraser, the folder. In our effort to help children learn to manage their things, we stifle their motivation to give. Don't hear me say, "Stop labeling those supplies," because there is a black hole in every classroom where crayons go to die. But what if we bought a box for our student and one to have handy for the child who has none? What if we did as much teaching about being ready to give generously as we do about keeping conscientiously?

Among the first words children learn to use before most fall into the category of a student, the word "Mine!" is both a label and a statement. Lessons are not needed for children to learn to keep good things for themselves. Keeping comes naturally, but giving is a practice we never stop learning.

God loves giving when giving is willing. Anyone can give with reluctance or because of force. God is fond of and pleased by giving produced by a joyful

18

heart wanting to give. When a child gets excited to bring a favorite fruit for a classroom snack, it's joyful giving. When a student wants to share crayons with a classmate who has none, it's cheerful giving. When a learner wants to bring a new folder for the tablemate whose folder was lost between houses, it's good giving. It's generous, and God loves it in a learner.

Digging Deeper

3 Ways to Give

- Look for invitations like can drives to give generously together.
- Notice and note when you see a need and talk about how you could help.
- Acknowledge when you have more than needed, give thanks, and talk to your student about who might need your excess.

Table Talk

- When we make a shopping list, what if we put something extra to give away?
- The Bible says God loves a cheerful giver. Why do you think He wants a giver to be willing?
- Can you think of someone who had a happy heart when they gave to you?

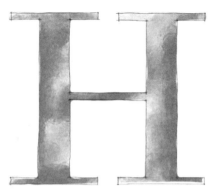

HUMILITY

"Do nothing from selfish ambition or conceit, but in humility count others more significant than yourselves. Let each of you look not only to his own interests, but also to the interests of others. Have this mind among yourselves, which is yours in Christ Jesus." - Philippians 2:3-5

The fight broke out in the lunch line beside me when drama swept up two girls on opposite sides of the cooler. I was just holding my tray, lost in the insecurity of puberty, unaware of what was about to happen. Before I could get out of the way, someone grabbed a milk carton, held it in place, and smashed it in a single, swift, exploding motion. Surprise diverted attention from the argument as milk poured down my head and face. Through a waterfall of white liquid, I saw looks of shock as snickers erupted into laughter. I ran dripping with milk out of the crowded cafeteria to the only refuge I could reach—the girls restroom.

Milk-soaked and crying, I hid myself, wondering how I would ever come back from such humiliation. News travels fast in middle school and clings long into high school. The door opened and another student entered, asking if I was okay, helping to clean the mess I hadn't made. She left her lunch and her uninvolved place in my nightmare to treat me more importantly than herself. She didn't laugh or talk about what happened. She helped. She set aside her own pubescent reputation to look out for my interests and become part of my embarrassment. When immature kids enter school with other immature kids, there's a good chance they will have a need or face humiliation. This single truth tempts us to shield our kids from interactions that may lead to such pain. Sooner or later, whatever their classroom context, every child encounters hardships on the way to growing a right sized perspective of self. A humble heart is the best deliverance out of humiliation.

It's natural to love ourselves. By the time a little one is six months old, they begin to enjoy seeing their own face in a mirror and respond to the sound of their own wonderful name. We right size our self-view when we open up our others-view to let them be important, even more important than we see our own concerns. To learn to "count" others more significant than ourselves is to have modesty, thinking about others in a way that stands out over our own needs and wants. This wise way of thinking means we have a modest opinion of who we are, instead of inflating our own importance.

God loves a humble heart in a child. He loved the humble heart of His own Son.

Jesus modeled perfect humility by putting our condition ahead of His, setting aside what He deserved, so He could meet our need caused by our sin. Instead of standing at a distance, refusing to soil Himself with our sin, He came down and accepted the limits of mankind so He could address our mess. When we couldn't get out of the way, He got in the way for us. The humble heart of Jesus was the deliverance for our humiliation.

In the face of failure, a humble heart provides comfort.
In the face of opposition, a humble heart provides strength.
In the face of loneliness, a humble heart provides companionship.
In the face of humiliation, a humble heart provides rescue.

Educational structures often reward achievers and champions. It's fulfilling to do our best, be enthusiastic, and work hard. Sometimes, our students will be honored, but sometimes, they'll be humiliated. They may be the cause of their circumstances, or they may simply find themselves on the wrong side of a cafeteria cooler. We walk a fine line as parents in urging growth, but not fueling an appetite for personal importance. There will be no lack of messages urging our student to be significant, but God loves the humble heart of a child who learns to look out for others.

God loved humility in the heart of His Son, and He loves it in the hearts of our kids too.

Digging Deeper

3 Ways to Pray

- If moments of humiliation come, would You provide a humble student to come alongside my child?
- When others suffer, would You prompt my child to see and respond to the interests of others?
- Would You help me talk more about the importance of humility than about increasing our own importance as parent or child?

Table Talk

- How can you take care of yourself at school, but also take care of others?
- What would someone act like if they thought they were really important?
- If we saw someone sad or hurting, how could we have a humble heart and help?

INITIATIVE

"Little children, let us not love in word or talk but in deed and in truth."

1 John 3:18

They warned me. He was known for producing trouble, but little work. His physical strength and academic struggles didn't help. Childish misunderstandings quickly lit his short fuse. How could a child with so much energy show so little initiative?

It wasn't long before Dustin assured me he was trying to do his best, and I believed him. We just needed to find out how he was wired to show it. In school, as in life, actions prove intentions. I needed to see results to verify Dustin's attempts at change, but this boy needed an invitation to something that would ignite his unique interests and abilities.

Information about the Air Force art contest came around the time I started seeing planes scribbled in corners of his worksheets. When I asked if he would like to enter the contest, his eyes lit with excitement. With his parents' permission, Dustin began to stay after class, working with colored pencils to fill the smooth, extra large art paper, never needing to be reminded or redirected. The blank canvas came alive with his imagination as the sky filled with colors, shapes, and clouds. We found the way he could demonstrate his desire to do his best within his unique design.

God's heart for our children is for them to learn to live for Him in actions, not just in words. Rather than just talking about doing or just wanting to do good, He wants them to do. Do what a follower of Jesus does.

A "deed" is a thing we undertake to accomplish. When we take initiative to accomplish things that please God, He wants it to be done in truth, to align with what's true in His eyes. Maybe this also means we take action in ways He uniquely designed us to function best. This could mean we skillfully, prayerfully, lovingly find the best way to invite our child to act in their uniqueness. As we help our children discover who God made them to be, we position them to become children of initiative.

When the news came that Dustin's entry won the contest, we celebrated his amazing artwork. More than that, we celebrated breaking free from the certainty he could not succeed. For the first time, this hard-to-ignite child discovered he is fearfully and wonderfully made, able to take initiative within his uniqueness and create something of value. His energy found expression and was met with admiration, and his reputation changed. Dustin was inspired to take initiative and do something wonderful.

Digging Deeper

3 Ways to Learn

- Watch your child to see what stirs motivation. How could this become an invitation to initiative? (Art, music, sports, reading, serving, memorizing, etc.)
- Listen to what your child talks about in detail or shares first. What does this tell you about their interests?
- Make a variety of activities available and see which your child chooses. When we study the way God made our kids, we help them grow in their design.

Table Talk

- If we had a silent dinner, how would we show what we want to say?
- What's a way to say you love someone, and what's a way to show it?
- Let's take initiative and show good behaviors without telling what they are. Then we'll guess what we were each doing. (sharing, helping, encouraging, waiting, praying, etc.)

JOYFULNESS

"Rejoice in the Lord always; again I will say, rejoice."

Philippians 4:4

She was one of the smaller ones, but her bright eyes and ready smile revealed resilience deep within. Thin gold curls framed a face usually wearing a calm expression. With a name like "Harmony," joyfulness was meant to reside in her heart and on her face. On the morning after the police took her daddy away, her joy was marred by a trembling lip giving away grief discovered. Her familiar expression took effort.

To "rejoice" is to be glad, really glad, and in a state of being calmly happy. It's a state of heart and mind so at home in a child. After all, joy is the juice of childhood.

But sometimes juice becomes bitter, and the joy our children are meant to know is spoiled by the things of life. No parent wants to cause spoiled joy, but sometimes we do, and other times, it's out of our control. Student years move our child's development from a place where growth mainly depends on what is done to them to a place where they want to set their own identity. From needing help tying shoes, to getting dropped off at football games, a gradual change takes place in the role parents play, and social influences grow in significance bringing challenges with it.

When Paul wrote to his Philippian friends, he helped them know how to practice joyfulness in the face of life's hardships. Like the pathway of a student in the early years of learning, selfishness and suffering can press into a naturally joyful spirit. With encouragement God is at work in us to help us "shine as lights" (Philippians 2:15) while we make knowing Jesus our aim, Paul the teacher turned the minds of his students to the place where joy remains. Above.

The normal challenges of childhood and uninvited trauma have a way of sucking the joy out of developing students. If we could protect our children from every pain and disappointment, we would, but we can't. Each one needs to discover the source of real strength leading to deep abiding joy. Always? Always is for all times, forever. Joy can live beyond temporary events scarring a heart with lasting pain. In this same letter about real reasons to need and find joy, Paul describes his journey of learning to be content, even if "brought low." Paul knows we can do all things through Christ who empowers us, because he walked his own journey of hard-won resilience to joy.

Harmony's mama didn't hide her pain as well as her young student. When she arrived for pick up, her own quivering lip dissolved in tears with eager acceptance of my open arms and offer to pray. A mother can't give her child what she has not received. If joy is to be sifted out of the rubble of our pain, it has to be rooted in peace outside of what we can wrap our minds around.

"Do not be anxious about anything, but in everything by prayer and supplication with thanksgiving let your requests be made known to God. And the peace of God, which surpasses all understanding, will guard your hearts and your minds in Christ Jesus." (Philippians 4:6-7)

Joy is the juice of childhood, but it can be spoiled. It can also be preserved. As children enter classrooms of peers with non-relative caregivers and educators, they need to know where resilient joy comes from. Educate their heart and mind at each developmental stage with the truth of heaven and the peace of God through His Son Jesus. That's where real, deep joyfulness comes from.

Digging Deeper

3 Ways to Keep Joy

- At each age, let your student process and share their hardships. Be empathetic about what pains them, but be encouraging about finding peace together. We want joyful children, but authentically joyful children.
- Check your own joyfulness. How are you living out a joyful life?
- Keep life light when you can. Let the joyful juice of childhood flow!

Table Talk

- Let's look at what joyfulness looks like on each other's faces.
- Sometimes it's really hard to be joyful. When is it hard for you?
- What's a joy stealer to look out for? How can we help each other in those times?

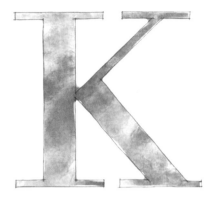

KNOWLEDGE

"An intelligent heart acquires knowledge,
and the ear of the wise seeks knowledge."

Proverbs 18:15

Our children need to get knowledge, but not just any knowledge. In God's design of human thinking capacity, children are naturally born to learn.

There's not a lot of finger painting in kindergarten anymore. In fact, children face a stream of more information than ever before when entering the school years. Current curriculums deliver vast amounts of academic content in aggressive plans of scope and sequence to ensure students make the grade and meet the benchmarks. With the arrival of the internet, there's no way students can know everything, yet they're challenged to know how to find what they need to know. Schedules have shifted to accommodate new standards of gaining knowledge.

The Zero to Three: National Center for Infants, Toddlers and Families* describes the remarkable rate of brain development between birth to age three, when a million neural connections form every second. Parents can help promote healthy brain development during the all important first five years and then in the formative years to follow. Good nutrition, adequate rest, positive social and emotional environments, and limited exposure to toxins like smoke build on a child's divine design to learn. Keeping chronic stress to a minimum and monitoring screen time seem like good parenting tactics, but they're also wise ways to build a healthy brain.

Touring a science fair or attending a spelling bee leaves no doubt knowledge wins in traditional schooling settings. Parents put in a lot of time drilling students in math facts and spelling words. A diagnosis of a learning disability may weigh heavily on a mom or dad who wonders if their child will ever be able to see, absorb, process, and recall all of the information presented as vital knowledge. But when knowledge fits in the larger picture of life, lessons encompass more than memorization.

Knowledge includes so much more than academic information. A lot of knowledge about unimportant things has the potential to stir up pride (1 Corinthians 8:1). Knowledge of God is something to be desired (Hosea 6:1). Knowledge begins with a reverence for God (Proverbs 1:7). Rejecting knowledge leads to destruction (Hosea 4:6-7). Knowledge is more about an "intelligent heart," able to understand and perceive what matters most, than it is about gathering massive amounts of information. "The wise" want knowledge that helps in deciding what's worthy to pursue, and that's the kind of knowledge we want for our students.

We can't know it all, so we discern what matters most to know.

Do the flash cards. Practice the spelling. Glorify God by winning that science fair! Or just love learning about the One who made the world and all the science in it. That matters more than the percent on the test or the grade on the report or the speed of multiplication. Let's raise today's standards beyond the scope and sequence in the curriculum. Let's aim for intelligent hearts and wise ears seeking to know the most precious things.

But what about the family Christmas letter or the trophy-sized space on the mantel? Every parent wants their child to succeed, to grow their potential, and to excel. We've been trained to believe and expect the best childhoods include trophies and awards. But every childhood is unique, and every child is unique. There are greater gains than shiny trophies, medals, or awards. "Gold there is, and rubies in abundance, but lips that speak knowledge are a rare jewel." (Proverbs 20:15, NIV)

Today's child needs to know a lot. Students need to get knowledge, but not just any knowledge. May they know God and want to know what matters most.

Digging Deeper

3 Ways to Know What Matters

- Children produce what parents applaud. Celebrate more than information or academics. Celebrate understanding things that matter most.
- Have books in your home about a wide range of subjects including creation, people, and spiritual truth. Be sure books fit your child's developmental stage.
- Make knowledge part of your regular conversation. Talk about what knowledge and understanding you are getting and why you care to get it.

Table Talk

- What's something new you learned today?
- If you could learn about anything, what would it be?
- What do you think is really important to know about?

*https://www.zerotothree.org/espanol/brain-development

LISTENING

"The way of a fool is right in his own eyes, but a wise man listens to advice."

Proverbs 12:15

Teachers train for such moments, but they hope the training won't be needed. A quick scan of the room registered in my mind that a grand mal seizure gripped Dawson's thin frame. Slow motion and speed seized the room at the same time. I dropped to the tile floor to clear his airway and tip his blonde head back while shouting, "Class, everyone stay in your seats. Nate, go to the office and tell them Mrs. Sanders needs emergency help right away. Dawson is having a seizure and we're going to take care of him!"

Foam overflowed onto his white cheeks. I fought back tears wanting to trickle down mine. There was no time for that. I sensed the concern and care of each watching child, yet all sat silently in place. Nate ran for them all to the office, returning with help for our treasured student and friend. After the blur of mere minutes, emergency workers arrived to take over, along with Dawson's overwhelmed mom. When they all left, the students gathered tight for the comfort of closeness to talk about what happened and how their wise listening helped Dawson, the medical team, and all of us. Their obedience saved our friend. Not in my curriculum that day, the class passed the listening lesson with flying colors when it mattered most.

No one knows when a crisis will strike, but when it does, we need to know our children will give attention obediently to what they're told. We need to know they'll listen. Students learn in a thousand small moments where they repeat the process of hearing, attending, and obeying. Coming when called, joining in a task, participating with a group, stopping to change course, or helping when invited. Listening.

As a child gives attention to advice in the common, they prepare to comply to commands in crisis.

A foolish way is the opposite of a careful and wise way. To be a wise person is to make a careful judgment about what you hear. Attentive listening produces cooperative action. The child who walks in the "way of a fool" thinks her chosen course looks correct, but the wise child hears and pays attention obediently. Messages may reach both children, but one resists, while the other receives.

Children are born with the desire to hear what's around them, so they know what to expect, how to respond, and how to be safe. No sooner are they out of the womb than they need to learn to sort sounds and determine what to give attention to and what to shut out. From their earliest days of responding to noise, we work with our little ones to teach them what needs to be heard. As new sounds and voices enter in and peer messages become more prominent, new practice is needed in how to tune in to what matters most and decide what can be trusted.

Grown ups train a child to tune in or tune out.

Effective listening says as much about the speaker as the listener. From the earliest days, children listen to find out if they can trust and if they can understand. They listen to find out if we follow through and if we are worth hearing. Parents who don't listen to their own communication may put all responsibility on children as the listeners and become an obstacle to obedient listening. By working at communicating in a clear, calm manner, we help students take the wise path of paying attention.

If we want our children to grow into wise listeners, we need to begin by listening.

- Listening to what God says about how we speak.
- Listening to what we sound like when we communicate.
- Listening to other parents who model wise speech.
- Listening to our partner who gives us feedback about our talk.
- Listening to our children to know if we're helping them or giving reasons to resist being a listener.

Lord Jesus, help my child to grow into a wise person who listens to advice.

Wise students learn to listen. Wise parents learn how to be heard, and that begins with listening. Grown ups train children to tune in or tune out.

Digging Deeper

5 Ways to Engage Listening

- Physically get down on a child's level. Use the child's name.
- Make eye contact and physical contact (Hold a hand, shoulder or a back).
- Speak in a steady, calm voice.
- Ask your child to repeat what they heard you say.
- Use communication with your child that you want your child to use with you.

Table Talk

- What do you look like when you are listening to me?
- What do you want me to do to show I'm listening to you?
- Sometimes it's hard to listen at school. What helps you be a listener there?

MATURITY

"Brothers, do not be children in your thinking. Be infants in evil, but in your thinking be mature."

1 Corinthians 14:20

Childhood is a pathway towards maturity, not to be hurried or hindered.

"Let's act our age," may come out of a parent or teacher's mouth at any stage on a child's pathway towards maturity. Potty jokes in second grade or sarcasm from a teenager only validate what we know; a child's brain isn't fully developed until at least age 25. The word "children" in 1 Corinthians 14:20 refers to a young person, even a baby. "Thinking" refers to our ability to perceive and judge what's true about life. Some say it takes even longer than twenty-five years to move from infancy through immaturity to independence. Truth is, independence isn't always an indicator of maturity.

To be like an infant is to be innocent. To be mature is to be grown completely in character. On the way to full moral growth, we hear a lot of bathroom humor, talking back, and childish thinking. While parents partner with teachers to guide student growth, a lot of childishness takes place as children do what they're made to do: act their age.

By definition, a student is someone who thoughtfully engages in learning, some in a formal program. Growth and change demonstrate increases in knowledge and understanding. The challenge to "in your thinking be mature" was written about learning to interact with different people, people with other gifts and abilities. Students today face exposure to a wider range of different people than ever before.

When exposure explodes, the maturity pathway may be hurried. For example, social media and technology have the potential to entice our maturing student before they're ready, offering a buffet of too much information without enough discernment. To ensure our student's pathway to maturity isn't hurried, we are wise to carefully consider our child's readiness for access to the larger world and for that world's access to our child. This is one way a parent thoughtfully ensures the pathway to maturity isn't hurried or hindered.

God provides guidance and wisdom for the mature parent, so childhood isn't derailed by premature exposure to adult ideas or concepts. Wise parents guide the pace of growing up based on their child's development and their family's values, not on decisions of the families around them. On the pathway to maturity, a parent helps to monitor the pace.

As children move through developmental stages or maturity, the ability to handle input changes. For example, in our highly stimulating world, attention is a moving target. In kindergarten, the average attention span lasts 10 to 15 minutes, but by third grade, a child may attend for 30 minutes. Parents see evidence of physical and mental milestones in a child's behaviors and words. The challenge is to support a well-paced pathway for each individual child, without hurry or hindrances.

Most parents waffle between wishing their child would stay little and wishing they'd hurry and grow up. We can't have it both ways. Sometimes our urges reflect our own growth and need for connection. If we let our desires drive our child's pathway to maturity, we may hinder their progress.

I painstakingly stitched brightly colored tools on a romper for our son Jacob, taking him to have his picture taken to mark his third birthday. But when he went to preschool the next year, my husband Jeff insisted it was time to leave the toddler rompers behind. When it came time to help that same boy move away to a new season on his formal program as a student, Jeff reminded me, "We raised him to be mature." Maturity is a gradual process that can't be hindered to satisfy a mother's delights.

It's possible to long for the days when our students were little, and for their maturity to face their future, at the same time. If we're honest, parenthood is a pathway towards our maturity too.

May God help us grow up as parents who shepherd our children on an unhurried, unhindered pathway to maturity.

Digging Deeper

3 Ways to Watch on the Pathway to Maturity

- Be alert to the pace of maturity. Know how much your child is ready for.
- Be informed about how parents of child peers pace their pathway to maturity.
- Be aware of personal temptations to keep children in childhood longer than God plans. Speaking from experience, friend, we can't stop that process!

Table Talk

- How do you know when someone is grown up?
- How does a baby act differently than a child? How is a teenager different?
- What does a baby have to learn to grow all the way to being grown up?

NEIGHBORS

"The second is this: 'You shall love your neighbor as yourself.' There is no other commandment greater than these."

Mark 12:31

I watched her heart wither without friends, much less neighbors. My relational girl craved connection, but a foreign culture and language made each conversation challenging. A neighbor is anyone we come across, anyone our students come across, in their growing up journey. A child's heart has a special niche where a neighbor needs to fit.

As a child's character grows more mature, the student becomes better equipped to consider the needs of others and show love as they want to be loved. To obey this commandment, a child needs to know their neighbor and practice loving. Jesus delivered this command after explaining the first, which is to love God. Being a good neighbor is the natural outcome of being a God-lover. A student encounters neighbors on the bus, in the hallway, in the classroom, on the playground, in the cafeteria, in the locker room. There will be no shortage of neighbors when children enter into a structure for learning with peers. The two-fold challenge includes creating connection with those they come across and applying skill in caring for them.

Knowing neighbors starts when a family creates a foundation for how to view and accept others outside the family. Gradually, children take approaches learned at home and put them into practice as they grow in social connections and independence. A six-year old enjoys sharing, but their developing imagination may conjure up an imaginary companion. The next year, the learner may embrace the idea of playing by the rules with others, before testing the stage of sharing their opinions and covering up their strong emotions. By the time a child celebrates an eighth birthday, learning leads to increased independence, looking back to adults as stabilizers, especially in moments of stress. After all, as children interact with more outsiders, loving neighbors increases the complexity of their widening world. Family systems create a framework to support growing children in readiness and skill to connect with and care for unrelated people—neighbors.

As neighbors fit into the special niche in a child's heart, moms may long for the days when it was easier to control the relational connections. But that would interfere with the process of maturity. Moms have to care for neighbors, so students will care for neighbors.

About the time my girl's hopes became an ache, a small dark head pushed her way through a hole in the wall, parting the long grass and following the path to our door. A neighbor. A neighbor came across us and reached out to be known from her shanty on the other side of the wall with the hole. Children in every place and culture are wired to know their neighbor.

And that's when my mama's heart had to lean into the commandment Jesus gave, the greatest commandment. Was it okay for my girl to go through the tall grass and into a hole in the wall? Can a mom make sure her still maturing learner can be safe while learning the lessons of a good neighbor? Children have incomplete discernment and need the stabilizing power of a loving parent as they practice being neighborly. God gives us wisdom to protect our growing students, without preventing their learning. Before long, the neighbor girls popped in and out of the cinder block wall to visit and play with each other, and other neighbors followed.

If the neighbor niche in a child's heart is to be occupied as planned, a mother has to open her heart as well.

Digging Deeper

4 Ways to Love a Neighbor

- Decide you will be friendly, not fearful. Introduce yourself to neighbor kids and families in your schooling journey. Use names and offer yours. Caring requires connection.
- Create an open home where neighbors can play, eat, or study. Be the open home and life where your student is welcome to bring others.
- Use a meal to create connection with a neighbor. Keep it casual and comfortable by breaking bread outside, at a park, or in a common area.
- As your child grows, step back to allow for their development, but stay present and informed. Love neighbor children as you want others to love yours.

Table Talk

- Jesus said to care as much about neighbors as we do for ourselves. Who do you think is our neighbor?
- How do you think a neighbor is the same or different than a friend?
- What would we need to do or say to help neighbors feel cared for?

OVERFLOW

"May the God of hope fill you with all joy and peace as you trust in him, so that you may overflow with hope by the power of the Holy Spirit" - NIV

Romans 15:13

If all our students had to encounter as they grow from child to adult was new information, it would be enough. But uncertainties surround the process of learning. Uncertainty about their changing self, their peers, their teachers, their futures, and our world. Stand and survey the river of student faces flowing through a high school hallway, or observe the expressions filing through a cafeteria line, and you will see uncertainty etched into lines of restraint and insecurity. It's normal to work out who we are and who we want to be, but the uncertain student longs to know where to place their trust.

If you've picked up *The ABC's of Praying for Students*, you must hope your child will know where to place their trust. At the same time, you might need your own reminders of where to place your trust. Watching the journey of childhood can hurt our hearts and leave us feeling uncertain. We know we can trust in the God of hope, but schooling reminds us how desperately we need Him.

We don't just want our kids to have enough hope for the morning, we want them to be filled up with joy and peace to overflow all day with empowerment. When children see what overflowing looks like, they know it's okay to let their own joy and peace spill over.

Charlotte came to first grade every week. She brought a new book discovered in her planned trips to the library, selections connected to the season or subject. My class included one of her lanky twins, a brilliant, but quiet boy moving between awkward stages of uncertainty and confidence. Towering above me, smiling Charlotte brought her joy down into our circle, settling into my rocking chair and leaning in as if she brought a precious gift to impart to the students. And she had.

With her bright, wide open eyes, our weekly guest reader opened colorful pages and read each with a variety of voices, hand motions, and excitement. Insecurity and restraint fell away as Charlotte modeled freedom and fullness for her son and his classmates. Fueled and filled by her own faith, this mama delivered joy into our classroom by reading a children's book to God's glory with an unleashed overflow. As she abounded in who God made her to be, she illustrated what the Holy Spirit's creativity looks like in us. Yet to be a mom myself, I watched and learned. Yet to be unleashed himself, her son watched and learned. When a mom abounds in hope, it's a beautiful thing.

Parenting is powerful when a mom learns to trust the God of hope so much it results in a joy and peace-filled overflow before her watching, learning child. The best way to help a child overcome the uncertainty of growing up is to model a life of joyful overflow.

Digging Deeper

4 Ways to Overflow

- Look for a need fitting your gifts and offer it in your child's school.
- Look for a need outside your comfort zone and trust God to help you do it.
- Look for a way to serve as a family or parent/child team, and joyfully tackle it.
- Ask God to give you a new opportunity and the joy and peace to go with it.

Table Talk

- Can you think of someone who does something with joy? How does it look?
- When we feel unsure, how can remembering what we believe about God help us feel powerful?
- What happens if we keep pouring water into a glass? What could we pour into our minds and hearts so hope and joy overflow from our life?
- How do you think a neighbor is the same or different than a friend?
- What would we need to do or say to help neighbors feel cared for?

PERSEVERANCE

"And let us not grow weary of doing good, for in due season we will reap, if we do not give up."

Galatians 6:9

Most great things happen over time and with great effort. Raising a child is one of those. By the time her mom reached out to find me, years had passed. A national talk show invited her to share about her daughter's personal journey of perseverance through a crippling anxiety disorder.

Everyone feels nervous the first day. But when Evelyn entered the room, she moved stiffly, with mechanical motions, forcing her body to bend into the chair. We barely engaged in welcomes, when a soft-hearted student drew close and spoke into my shoulder. "Mrs. Sanders, Evelyn can't talk. She never does at school. I can help." Evelyn's eyes agreed and eagerly accepted the intervention and offer to be her voice. Her jaw extended and her tongue stretched long in her mouth, worried eyes looking away, unblinking. Her twisting fingers exposed the urge to hold on to something. It would take time and great effort for great things to happen.

That year I watched as the soft-hearted friend continued to do good. I observed, read, learned, and tried whatever I could to understand and support Evelyn. Her mom wrestled as only moms do, but she did not give up wrestling. Half-hidden whispers became victories, and art therapy produced avenues for communication. One-on-one time allowed privacy for the painful work of learning to trust and move words from thoughts to tongue while in school. Evelyn did not give up.

We don't pray for or expect the same harvest in the lives of different students. Just as children encounter unique obstacles and adversity, so they discover personal pathways around those barriers. Reaping a harvest requires the passage of time and perseverance in trials.

Perseverance pushes through the hardest things and the longest things to get to the best things. Parent or student, no one else feels a burden exactly like we do. Hardships have a way of sucking away at strength and optimism. Students learn this unwelcome lesson while encountering daily, or even moment by moment, trials. Fatigue is a natural byproduct of those battles, but perseverance means we hang on and we hold on, even when we can't see how long the battle will be.

To "grow weary" is to become exhausted and weak. At our lowest, our spirit may "fail" in our very heart of hope, leading to deep discouragement. Students are not immune from this, despite the shelter of childhood. Motherhood has its way of bringing moms to moments like these. We must resist the urge to provide premature rescue from hard things for our students. We may need accountability to help our kids hold firm, instead of giving in to our personal pain in watching them wrestle. Parents ache while watching students suffer through a science project, stick to a therapy plan, stay with a class schedule, or finish out a season. Students need support to hang on through adversity, not permission to avoid it.

"Due season" is the "right time," once time passes and the harvest reaper refuses to relax determination.

Time passed daily with Evelyn's efforts to calm her anxious spirit, bring her rigid fingers into submission, make her tongue yield to her thoughts, and stir her courage to match her determination. She did not give up, until she stood before hopeful peers in the spring and softly read aloud from her journal. The soft-hearted friend beamed. It was a shared victory.

Evelyn still didn't give up, because great things take time and warriors keep trying. She persevered beyond spring and into a frightening new classroom again and again. Reaping a harvest sounded like laughing with friends and looked like raising her hand to answer out loud and, of all things, talking out loud to compete in a spelling bee! It was a great thing, and the story of her victory and those who refused to give up was a story to tell. That's why her mama called me. The mother of the little girl who did not give up would also not give up, until she found me in a new state and told me of the harvest she and Evelyn celebrated from the seeds we had sown.

Every student needs to be an overcomer. As they persevere, we must persevere in allowing our learners to gut it out through the hard moments, days, and years to reap a harvest. It will take time and great effort for them and for us, and great things will happen.

Digging Deeper

3 Questions to Ask to Support Perseverance

- Can you help me know what makes this really hard and how you feel about it?
- When we persevere through this, what will success look like for you?
- How can I help you not to give up?

Table Talk

- What song could you sing in your head if you're doing something hard?
- What kind of an animal would you want to have as a pet, if you had a hard job to do that would take a long time?
- What kind of a friend would you want to have with you, if you had to do something hard for a long time, but you knew it would turn out to be great?

QUIET

"A fool gives full vent to his spirit, but a wise man quietly holds it back."

Proverbs 29:11

Over the weekend I twirled and flipped at the playground, until my fingers slipped and I fell hard. Despite my seven year old bones, my bruised back ached until Monday morning. I'm still not sure why I told her, since she was not the kind of teacher to want to know. Maybe I wanted her to know my weekend world, just a little. When I told her about the flip and fall, she peppered me with questions. Decades later, I still remember her rising tone, angry eyes, and wagging finger. Didn't I know school grounds weren't for play outside school hours? I didn't know, and my lip quivered harder and my eyes spilled tears until I heard myself sputtering out loud. Her anger grew for reasons I didn't understand. In disgust, she called my mom. Embarrassed and confused about why my injury incited ire instead of interest, I left feeling like a fool.

Student life moves children from ignorant to thoughtful in the process of learning not to be a "fool." The strong word describes someone who is dull and even "stupid." That's a description moms put on the "off limits" list of vocabulary we know and don't use. If a child stays stuck in such a condition, emotions cut loose in a foolish way. This is the Bible's description of a full on meltdown.

Honest moms testify of having a moment or two on the journey of parenthood when they fell into a fool's vent. Life has a way of giving reasons to let extreme emotions out. Wisdom has a way of helping us express emotions in healthier ways than full on venting.

We aren't born wanting to hold back. From the earliest years, children discover tantrum power, especially when well-timed or well-placed. By the time childhood delivers kiddos to the student years, emotions are more sophisticated. Still, traumatic events and experiences collect inside a student's spirit, the seat of the emotions, begging for expression. Children want their deepest needs to be known, yet may not have discernment to know where and when to share. They may naively blurt out what's on their mind, discovering too late that the audience wasn't accepting.

When expression meets exposure, a student's emotions may erupt. Depending on the individual and setting, responses may swing from anger to confusion, embarrassment to hurt. At such moments, may God lead our learners to self-soothe in a way that holds back their torrent of emotion in healthy ways. This takes skill and self-regulation of the emotional response set in the fabric of being human. As children mature, they learn how and when to think through strong thoughts and feelings, including how and when to let them out. Holding back without healthy expression isn't healthy.

Children are feelers who become learners and decision makers. They decide what to do with big emotions surging through every stage, from early learning to senioritis.

- How should I manage these strong feelings right now in this place?
- Who is a safe person to tell about how I'm feeling?
- Who will help me understand my thoughts and emotions?
- How much of these strong feelings do I let out and at what rate?
- When is a good time to work through these big emotions?
- If I shouldn't stuff these thoughts, what do I do with them?

Just because a child receives a negative response to legitimate emotions doesn't mean those emotions are wrong. Becoming "wise" as a manager of our God-designed passion set includes learning to hold back until the right time and place.

I left second grade that day in choking tears and humiliation. My teacher didn't know what to do with my big feelings. She sent me home with bigger feelings than I started with. Like many things in student life and in parenting, it didn't start as a big deal, but it turned into one. Students encounter emotions in their one-of-a-kind way, and so do moms.

Let's mature beyond meltdowns and manage the big emotions of life.

Digging Deeper

3 Ways to Cultivate Quiet

- Look at your own emotions. Are you holding back until the right time and place?
- Use descriptive words to help your child identify and understand emotions.
- Include your feelings in your prayers, helping children know God wants to hear how we feel. With Him, we don't have to hold back.

Table Talk

- Take turns showing an emotion on your face to see if others can guess it.
- Share the steps you take when a big wave of feeling builds. Take a deep breath? Close your eyes? Go for a walk?
- Let each person share what they find helpful to manage a meltdown.

RESPECT

"Love one another with brotherly affection. Outdo one another in showing honor."

Romans 12:10

Milk sloshed in the plastic pitcher gripped in his small hands. I held my breath, hoping for success, but ready for clean up. The four year old carefully filled his cup before turning with a triumphant smile, offering milk to his neighbor. Around the table, preschoolers passed diced peaches, triangle shaped quesadillas and bowls of ranch dressing to their neighbors. Pride spilled over as they served each other under my watchful, slightly nervous gaze. The teacher chatted with her students without worry, gently guiding and supporting as needed, comfortable in letting the rhythms of respect roll out before our eyes.

As hungry children gobbled up lunch, requests for seconds came couched in "please" and "thank you," and classmates happily worked to be sure everyone was served. Since I was the guest at the table, it all appeared before my eyes to be a routine filled with hazards and risks. When a tipped cup emptied a pool onto the table, small friends reached with eager hands to help, until at last, the preschool students scraped their plates and stacked the empty bowls to clear the tables. Helpers used rags to corral pieces of peaches that didn't make it onto plates and to mop up milk rings where cups had been. Even the youngest students learn to savor the rhythms of respect.

As the program director, I know many of our children came from homes where mealtimes don't happen around tables. For some, mealtimes don't happen at all. By the time a child enters the world of peers and lessons, too many have heard and seen harsh words, angry actions, and rude reactions. They're hungry for food and so much more. I love visiting classrooms with meals served family-style and teachers gather with students around tables serving more than nutritious food to feed the hearts of the hungry. Some children came from families facing food insecurity, making it hard to imagine offering limited portions to others around the table. Even in the early learning years, children are hungry for more than a meal. They crave the love of their neighbors and the respect of their friends.

"Love one another with brotherly affection." The window of opportunity is open during childhood to feed a child's God-crafted craving to be treated with respect and to respect.

Loving one another with brotherly care means cherishing someone like family, with a mutual quality of tenderness that comes from believing each person has value. This sisterly or brotherly love can be learned, and it sets the standard for how followers of Jesus Christ treat each other as part of God's family. To "outdo" each other is more than doing the best job of loving. It's showing the way to lovingly care for each other by going first.

Instead of waiting for a neighbor, friend, or family member to deserve honor, a respectful heart takes initiative to act lovingly. There's no better place for a learner to practice this lesson than in their home. As parents take initiative to show the way to loving care in words and deeds among family, the rhythms of respect become etched into a child's sense of what's good. A student's family is the table around which they learn rhythms of respect to repeat as their world expands.

This directive to love with family-style tenderness in order to show the way to respect and honor comes inside a passage pointed at how authentic Christians show authentic love. Love is, after all, an action, so, "Let love be genuine. Abhor what is evil; hold fast to what is good," (Romans 12:9). As the world around our students teaches their ways, learners won't need to look far to see selfishness, and they won't need to listen carefully to hear arrogance. Evil will be easy to find and recognize, once students know how the standard of love looks and sounds. Pushing away evil and holding tightly to what is good will take determination; it will take a love for the rhythms of respect.

Not every child has the opportunity to know, love, and practice early lessons in respect. For some, unselfish actions delivered with kind words and honoring attitudes will be unfamiliar. Treating someone else with value, even preferring their needs above your own, may feel foreign. Their gnawing hunger may make them greedy or rude. But even they can learn to love like a family who loves.

If we long for our children to become students who treat others with honor, we can show them the way by reflecting respect with our family at home. A little spilled milk is a small price to pay for mastering the rhythms of respect.

Digging Deeper

3 Ways to Reinforce Respect

- Take turns serving each other at meals, not letting extra mess hold you back.
- Value the use of "You first." Say, "I hope I hear someone use 'You first' today!"
- Point out when a child puts someone else first, waits for their turn, or shows love in action just because it's good.

Table Talk

- How does it look when a student is full of respect to a teacher at school?
- What makes it hard to be respectful to others your age? People older than you?
- We can ask to be given more food in a respectful way or in a non-respectful way. What could non-respectful sound like? How could respectful sound?
- When someone talks to you disrespectfully, how does it make you want to respond? How is it different if they talk to you respectfully?

SELF CONTROL

"For this very reason, make every effort to supplement your faith with virtue, and virtue with knowledge, and knowledge with self-control, and self-control with steadfastness, and steadfastness with godliness, and godliness with brotherly affection, and brotherly affection with love."

2 Peter 1:5-7

It's not easy to find substitutes, especially when a class isn't easy. The two teachers in one unique class needed a break. Traditional classroom rules didn't make sense in their space where students weren't learning traditional lessons. Instead, clustered high needs required individualized curriculum, approaches, and plans to address a range of diagnosed concerns. The mix made it challenging for the team to find substitutes for their own normal needs and days off. Once they knew I was willing and able to help, I became their regular sub.

Early each day, I received essential information by listening to the daily routine. "Do you know your goal?" the teacher would ask. "I know my goal," each answered before the group, declaring their most important objective for the day. Goals were written at the front, where eyes turned often for reinforcement. Each student focused on mastering their own urges and emotions. Without self-control, the knowledge they wrestled to gain was incomplete.

School structures do a lot to help students succeed in getting knowledge. Schedules revolve around balancing time in certain subjects. The calendar bends to testing knowledge gained. Awards go to those who best recall information. In a group where students know they won't get all the content or give back all the answers, there's a beautiful balance in looking at the bigger picture. Do you know your goal?

The larger goal of developing character is worth making "every effort." Settling for just one quality would be a loss of what God intends for each learner. As faith grows, goodness results, leading to an open mind to understand. Planned learning is all about increasing knowledge. Without mastering the urges and emotions co-directing a child along with their informed thinking, all that data might just create a lopsided learner. Taking personal charge of the passionate side of our self is essential if we're to make it from faith to love without being derailed.

Life gives us reasons to be full of passion— good and bad. "Do you know your goal Matthew?" the teacher asked. "I know my goal," he answered, saying he would slow down and use words for his strong feelings. It was a singular objective on a day when he would engage what would feel like volumes of content. In short, he would exercise self-control. Knowledge mattered, but control mattered more.

Sitting across the table from me, I felt his urges escalating as we talked. The lead teacher moved closer, reminding Matthew of his goal for the day. All seemed well until the suffering student snapped, lunging at me over his workbook. After all was contained and quiet again, the students went to lunch, giving the teacher an opportunity to explain. What did I do to trigger that response? Nothing. I couldn't have known my voice was a carbon copy of the child's mother's voice, a voice reminding him of pain and heartache when her lack of self-control got in the way of love. It wasn't the information that set off the student's strongest emotions; it was injury caused by the uncontrolled emotions of the someone who mattered most.

Do you know your goal? My goal today is to live out the life I want my learner to live. On the way to achieving that objective, I'll gather information, practice, and make every effort in my head. Without self-control as a parent, all I know in my head won't make a difference in my child's heart. As students grow, all the head knowledge won't make a difference in the heart knowledge.

Self-control is the mechanism moving students from knowing to doing.

Classroom settings today encounter more challenges than ever before when it comes to self-control and children. Teachers struggle to help learners master content, because big behaviors get in the way of teaching. When children come to educational environments with emotional injuries, it's hard to care about information. Matthew was right about the goal mattering most for him that day. The beauty in that "special" class was in listening to the bold, honest declarations of students who identified their personal challenges with simple truth. What if each child approached each day with a statement of their goal for the day? Not just the knowledge-getting goal from their growing goodness, but their self-control goal of learning to master urges and emotions that come with being human in a human world.

At the end of every day, students provided a self-report. Peers shared observations, feedback, and encouragement with "brotherly affection" bringing a kind of love into the laboratory of learning. Each person set a new goal for tomorrow, because that's what we do when we keep learning and growing. It's worth every effort to complete growing in knowledge with growing in self-control.

Digging Deeper

4 Ways to Strengthen Self-Control

- Ask a simple question to start the day: Do you know your goal?
- At the end of the day, ask your student to share an example of when they achieved their goal and when they didn't achieve their goal.
- Talk about a goal you have for yourself, giving an example of when you accomplished your goal and when you didn't accomplish our goal.
- Be sure to include your goal in your prayer. Keep the language simple and honest, so it's memorable all day.

Table Talk

- Have you seen someone lose control? What did their face look like?
- How is our mealtime different because we show self-control with each other?
- How do you think self-control could lead to showing love?

THANKFULNESS

"Oh give thanks to the Lord, for he is good; for his steadfast love endures forever!"

1 Chronicles 16:34

Her stained dress barely covered her thighs. Lifting her fragile fingers to write in her journal took a lot of energy. Trini peeked out from beneath a wispy curtain of baby soft hair, exposing eyes heavy with hope, but cautious from experience. Learning to read was a lot to ask for a little girl with such big burdens. After searching for a way to motivate her effort, the principal granted special permission to let Trini set goals leading up to a weekend lunch date as a reward. Ignited by promise, she tried and worked and learned until a lunch date was set.

As I walked across their broken porch, I could see her mama looking out from a gauzy gray piece of curtain. I stepped into the drafty space where mostly darkness filled sparse rooms. Trini tucked her hand into mine, eager to find the "good" promised to her. At a local diner, tucked into a row of dormant shops on Main Street, we slid into a booth and Trini worked to read the menu. She had never been out to eat before, so every discovery drew a gasp of delight until she was laughing aloud. Fingering the silverware arranged before her, the little receiver pushed back her glasses and looked up to direct an important message to me. "This place is beautiful! It's the nicest place I ever been! Thank you for bringing me here. This is like heaven!"

Children are given to giving thanks. Even when facing want or encountering daily deficits, children are programmed for appreciation. Born needing to have every need met, little ones respond with a smile or laughter or unrestrained nuzzling to express their joy at being a receiver of good things. Thankfulness overflows in its earliest forms.

So why does it seem like students lose the skill of appreciation? Entering into an environment filled with peers presents a wide range of lifestyles and possessions, opportunities and potential. As a student's world expands, so does their awareness of what other "good things" are out there and who has them. Even one of the commandments warns of wanting what others possess. Jealousy and coveting robs a child of their contentment. Losing our sense of satisfaction leads to losing our attitude of appreciation.

Children are given to giving thanks, so give them lessons in thanksgiving. Schooling opens up opportunities for students to receive good things alongside others receiving good things. Just look across the table, at the next desk, into the other locker, or down the aisle. Comparison sets in. Some children come hungry, while others know only plenty. Giving thanks is a skill to cultivate intentionally, reinforcing contentment, while regulating comparison.

Since "Every good gift and every perfect gift is from above," (James 1:17) getting goodness presents a time for parents to teach the lesson of lifting thankfulness in the proper direction. What parent doesn't love receiving appreciation and honor from their child? It's right and good for children to acknowledge their parent's provision, but it's only a first step. "Oh give thanks to the Lord," means praise and gratitude are given in God's direction. Thanksgiving goes to the Person who ultimately provides. The youngest mind sees only the person across the table in the same booth, but as students grow, they understand how an unseen God lovingly gives every good thing. Trini was right to think of heaven when receiving her good things.

God deserves to have praise directed His way, because goodness and loving-kindness define His nature and last into forever. He knows when lifting a pencil or learning to read feels too heavy. He knows when motivation falters and life leaves a child fearful. He knows what Trini needs and what the student beside Trini needs. He knows what Trini's mama needs in her life behind the gray torn curtain. He knows, and He's working to keep and care for each one as He calls them to think of heaven and every good thing that comes from there.

As students face differences in the benefits of life, parents provide a model of contentment leading to appreciation expressed to the One from Whom all good things flow. While we teach the skill of showing thankfulness to people who serve and give, true thankfulness grows when we take teaching to the next level and direct gratitude to God Himself, the Giver of all good things.

Children are given to giving thanks, so give them lessons in thanksgiving.

Digging Deeper

3 Ways to think about Thankfulness

* Thankfulness pours from the heart and into our habits. Simply say, "Thank you" as an example inside and outside your home.
* Take opportunities to say thankfulness prayers of praise to God at the moment He gives good things. Students learn best "in the moment."
* Be aware of giving or having too much, so your child's natural urge to express gratitude isn't exhausted in an environment of excess.

Table Talk

* Who did God use to deliver a good thing to you today?
* What other words can we use to describe being thankful?
* When we say thank you, what are we saying about the giver? What if it's God?

UNDERSTANDING

"The unfolding of your words gives light;
it imparts understanding to the simple."

Psalm 119:130

I flipped through old report cards and certificates, evidence of childhood when days were simpler. From deep in the box, I pulled a copy of *Monster on the Bus,* a worn book with a water colored purple monster. Still smiling, he reminded me of how confusing school can be. I loved the motivating Monster books, so it took no time at all for me to read that one in the leveled readers series of my first grade year. When I tried to turn it in for the next one, the teacher declared, "Impossible! You can't be done!" But I was done. It was that simple. "You think you're done? Well, keep reading it." Out of fear of another "Impossible!" I did keep reading. I read and read over and over until I didn't know what to do with *Monster on the Bus.* In danger of moving to the struggling readers group, I decided Monster should disappear so I could move on with everyone else! Being a student is not always simple. Sometimes it's hard to understand.

In each stage of our student's pursuit to grow more and to know more, understanding poses an obstacle on the pathway to progress. In my first grade mind, it was the difference between literal and figurative language, not to mention discerning when to self-advocate and when to submit. I opted for the safe route, which plunged me into a black hole called *Monster on the Bus.* By the time learners reach upper elementary, the quest to understand may be about distinctions and differences between boys and girls. In middle school, students attach words like "Algebra" with effort and persistence to understand, before moving into high school where broader subjects like Physics complicate matters before bigger questions like life direction enter in. The pursuit of understanding encompasses both content and character in the education of our learners.

The degree of grit a student invests in getting knowledge directly impacts their gain. But understanding is a different subject altogether than gaining knowledge. To understand is to move from recognition of definition to the realization of application. It's going from translating the words "Keep reading it" into obedient repeated readings to careful consideration of whether or not the whole story of Monster riding a bus has been covered, processed, and comprehended. True understanding moves a student to proper action, possibly action requiring greater courage and commitment than simple obedience. I'm embarrassed to say it took weeks and countless readings for childhood me to figure out my teacher's misunderstanding and come up with a way around it. It wasn't the best way around it, but I moved on. I suppose I left an impression with my teacher that *Monster on the Bus* was a real beast for me. She didn't understand.

We never stop needing to ask for understanding, because we're much quicker to speak than to listen and to say we know than to ask a question. Well-meaning adults can be so guilty of this. Our inner child always needs to understand. How beautiful that in the simplicity of childhood, students know they need to understand. Before we taint their minds with training, turning them to believe they don't need to understand, we can help them to learn the way of those who seek learning illuminated with light.

What God teaches in the Bible, His Word, gives understanding. It helps us know who made us, why He made us, and what He made us for. It helps us to know how complex and intentional creation is, making us learners in the laboratory of divine design. Childhood is the season when the simple soak up understanding before hitting the obstacle of arrogance.

By opening God's truth in relevant ways to match what students encounter in their experience, we lead them in the way of those who seek illuminated learning. We embrace asking questions. We lean in close to listen. We wait to tell, because we long to hear. We grow in awareness beyond ourselves. We seek to see what else God made so we can know Him. In a dark world, we strain to gain understanding by the light of what God tells us is true. Though we are simple, He wants us and our children to be students of understanding.

I still have my copy of *Monster on the Bus*. I keep it with my report card that says my reading was "Satisfactory." In first grade, that bothered me. Now I understand. I know what God says about me, and I'm glad to be counted among the "simple."

Digging Deeper

3 Ways to grow Understanding

- Get in the habit of asking before telling. Use a simple beginning like, "I wonder" or "I'm curious about."
- It's wonderful when our learners have conversations with us about what they know. Ask, "I wonder what else we need to know."
- As a child becomes more aware of the world, use their discoveries to find out what God says. "Let's see what the Bible says about that."

Table Talk

- What do you think you understand better today than yesterday?
- Is there something you hope you understand better tomorrow?
- When you're grown up, what do you hope you understand most?

VICTORY

"For by you I can run against a troop and by my God I can leap over a wall."

Psalm 18:29

The red-haired boy made sure everyone knew he was fast. Annual Presidential Physical Fitness tests proved it with official timers and score keeping. In our school, where boys and girls competed separately, it never occurred to me that winning times would be known, much less compared. But the red-haired boy found out. Tom Marshall couldn't believe my time beat his in the infamous shuttle run on the blacktop, but it did. After he cried out angry tears behind the brick gym wall, he sent a representative to notify me and my band of ladybug catching gal pals that I had been challenged to a run off. I was horrified. When the time came for the gym teacher to blow the whistle, my panic made me run faster. Tom was humiliated. The Laurel Ridge playground girls squealed in triumph. I beat Tom Marshall fair and square in front of the entire second grade. He was broken, and I could see it as I flipped my braids in a winner's swagger.

I'll admit, it felt good. "He never should've challenged me," I thought, "as if he was so sure I couldn't be faster." Why did he assume the timer was broken for me, but working for him? I showed him! No sooner did the cheering die down from my giddy girl group than I realized I didn't feel so good. It was a bitter victory.

We don't just want victories for our students. We want good victories born out of the best gifts God etched into their singular designs. We want victories to cultivate character making our children rise to their highest heights to point to and glorify the One Who gave them the gifts. Childhood is rocky ground for victories to take hold in young hearts, until they learn to navigate the pitfalls of pride. It can feel good to win. Winning feels good enough to want to keep winning, and that desire requires understanding, humility, and wisdom to grow up alongside it.

Since students encounter all manner of battles, competitions, and challenges in their education, each will have their chance to step up to the line to show themselves and the world what they bring to the race of life. None of our students want to come in last. No one wants to lose. Because children begin with a bent to please parents, we have the first opportunity to reinforce and reward the pursuit of victory. This changes as they develop, so we need to feed this in the early years. We want students to succeed when they try to "run against a troop" and "leap over a wall," whatever that troop and wall may look like.

More than simply being victorious, we want our children to engage their greatest challenges with God's help and for His pleasure. "For by you" means their Maker is the One who gave their gifts to run and leap or count or speak. As students come to their line to pursue victory, whatever their battle may be, they have victories and defeats. We would never choose failure for our warriors, but God knows they need it. Red-haired Tom Marshall must've needed it on the blacktop that day, and I needed it another day.

Your student already has a desire to do battle and be declared the victor; God planted that hope in their heart. Have you seen it? I saw it when my twenty first graders cheered hysterically as the tug-o-war ribbon crossed our classroom line, giving us victory. I saw it when my third grader clenched his fists in intense effort during his first spelling bee. I saw it when my teenager raced her mount down the ring in wild pursuit of a distant barrel.

God said your student is wonderfully made (Psalm 139:14). The heart of your learner wants to win at what makes him or her wonderful. Who's the troop to race? Where's the wall to leap over? What's the challenge to overcome? Get behind them? Absolutely! But your student needs more than you to win at being all they're created to be. They will run their best race in God's strength, for His pleasure, and towards His plan.

That's sweet freedom, and that's victory!

Digging Deeper

3 Ways to Victory

- Acknowledge ways God has gifted others you know, and give Him credit.
- Use your gifts as examples to tell how God made us to honor Him.
- Use words to teach your child to recognize races: challenge, battle, obstacle, race, test, competition. What other words describe your child's challenges? "This is a …. and God will help you do your best to leap over it."

Table Talk

- Did you see anyone win or lose today? How do you think they felt?
- What do you think is the best kind of race for you to run?
- How do you think it helps us to win? How does it help us to lose?

WISDOM

"But the wisdom from above is first pure, then peaceable, gentle, open to reason, full of mercy and good fruits, impartial and sincere."

James 3:17

He reached the trash can just in time. The classroom of strangers looked on, and the unfamiliar teacher tried to comfort the sick, new student. My new student. Before he left for school, my youngest told me he didn't feel well. I assured him it was normal to feel nervous going to a new school, especially mid-year. Don't good moms encourage kids to boldly do new things? Change stirs up our emotions, I told him. He would relax and feel better once he got there.

But he didn't. When I retrieved him from the office, pale and hot, his soaked shirt wreaked with evidence I made the wrong call. Moms need bucket loads of wisdom in the school-mom journey, even as students need wisdom in their student journey.

We do the best we can every time, but how do we know what's best?

Wisdom is about taking the perspective of the human and the divine and aligning them, based on experience and knowledge, to determine the best course of action. In the third chapter of James, wisdom comes in the context of interaction with people. It's about getting along. Wisdom fits into the part of life where actions move life towards peace. By conduct and conversation reflecting Christ, we create a more peaceful life. To parent our students without considering this, we take our family into a place of conflict.

When it comes to decision-making, we do our best to choose the wise path with the information we have. We rarely have all the information. Should we let him read that book? Should we let her go to that sleepover? Should we do both sports or one? Should we encourage that friendship? Should we sign up for that class? Should we schedule a meeting with that teacher? What's the wise course to take in the circumstances we're given?

During the school-age years, acceptance by peers grows more important. As adolescence approaches, children might experiment with how their family standards align with standards of their peer group. Friendships during this same period expand from what has typically included their own gender to include friends of the opposite sex. These changes create new scenarios for navigating the possibilities. At the same time, students may experience pressure to fit in. Students begin to think for themselves about aligning their decisions between the human and the divine. They may not know that's what they're doing, but they're trying to figure out what's wise based on what they desire and what they know is best. Every student faces choices about what they want and what's wise.

Our kids do the best they can every time, but how do they know what's best?

Since a student's decisions fall so frequently into the category of friendships, turning to James 3 for guidance makes sense. In teaching learners how to think about how God's ways fit with our instincts, we get practical help by reading what the Bible says about how we think and act towards others and how we use our words and manage our actions. God doesn't leave us wondering what we need to know for actions we need to take.

This is one reason it's so important that, in addition to learning academics, we take responsibility to ensure our learners are educated in the essentials of God's truth. The Bible provides God's perspective for life, so children need to develop familiarity with its format and content at an early age. Instead of letting it fall into the category of general books in life, God's word is the core guidebook for life. Through intentionally teaching students about stories of the real events and people in God's story, we prepare them to see how His story shapes their story. By making scripture memory a habit in our home, we engrain words of wisdom in our learner's heart and mind to act as guideposts for education and experience. Students need to make choices knowing how the divine lines up with daily decisions. In His word, God gives students His heavenly perspectives for their worldly problems.

Digging Deeper

3 Ways to Wisdom

- When a moment of decision comes, make it a habit to ask, "What would be the wise choice?"
- Identify the heavenly perspective and the general information coming together in a decision.
- Point out wise choices and results. Simply say, "That was a wise choice."

Table Talk

- What decisions did you have to make today?
- When was the last time you made a wise decision? How do you know it was wise?
- When was the last time you think you made an unwise decision? How did you know it was unwise?

EXCELLENCE

"Honor the Lord with your wealth and with the firstfruits of all your produce."

Proverbs 3:9

Woven throughout my schooling, I heard different versions of the intention found on many classroom walls. "We do our best every day." My mom called it out from behind me, "Do your best," as a reminder of the thing I should do all the time, every time. And that's what I tried to do. Hoping to please those who set the high bar, I bought in to the belief and made striving for excellence my only option. Once the standard became embedded in my thinking about each new day, it was hard to leave behind. What would happen if I didn't do my best? What value would I have if I was "less-than-best?" It was exhausting, and I dragged that burden into motherhood. A lot of moms can relate.

Parents want students to be all they can be. But maybe doing our best every day is unrealistic, even unsustainable. Instead, excellence may be more about learning when and why to do our best, instead of reaching the highest bar every time.

Rather than indoctrinating our students with the expectation to always strive for the high bar, a better lesson for life may be learning to discern who and what deserves our best.

First, only One is worthy of our best. Our "wealth" refers to the abundance we have. Firstfruits stand out from the sum total of what we produce, because they are the first yield of work we create. To show honor to the Lord, the Source of what we have, by using it specifically for Him is to trust that more will come for our needs. This challenge to give God our best comes inside a familiar passage about trusting "in the Lord with all your heart," (Proverbs 3:5-6). He deserves to be trusted because of His perfect character and the excellent expression of that character. He showed us His authentic love by giving His Son to provide for our best future.

The One who gave our energy, gifts, and abilities to do our work deserves to get the cream of the crop of what we produce. When we know who empowers us to do our best, we recognize and glorify Him by giving our best. Anytime we invest resources of effort and energy into striving for excellence, the Lord is worthy of receiving the credit. No doubt students bring joy to parents, family, and teachers when they make the most of their potential, but our Creator ultimately gets the glory from the good they do.

Excellence doesn't look the same for everyone. In spite of a parent's efforts, obstacles like learning disabilities, changes, peers, and the educational environment intersect to shape what it means for a child to trust in Jesus for help. Trust takes place within the framework constructed by a student's own design and set of circumstances. While the receiver of our trust may be the same Person, the route of our trusting is personal.

Honoring God looks infinitely unique in the singular people God has crafted. No two students are the same, so excellence and best-doing are equally diverse in their expression. Test scores, benchmarks, and syllabi may deceive children into believing the same bar measures excellence for all, but striving for excellence is an infinitely personal endeavor.

Is it true that, "Everything we do should have quality stamped all over it"? Whatever we do, we should, "do all to the glory of God," (1 Corinthians 10:31b), but we shouldn't do everything. We can't do everything, and trying to do everything without limitations is a fast track to burnout and collapse. To honor God by making sure He gets our best resources and our best results, we have to protect space and time in our lives to make way for His ways.

Countless options press into life, clamoring for a portion of our limited attention and commitment. Students learn to choose by watching and listening to the life we raise them in. They know what we genuinely consider to be our "wealth" and our "firstfruits" by seeing how we live inside the privacy of our parenting. We may maintain an appearance of excellence, while living a private life of exhaustion.

As our students watch and observe the most influential demonstration project in their education—our lives, we want them to learn a pattern they can follow. We can't do it all, shouldn't try to do it all, and can't do it the best every time. To keep up a life of authentic excellence, we need to choose what and who deserves our best efforts. First, we give Him our best.

Digging Deeper

3 Ways to Excellence

- Time check. How much time is God getting in your schedule? Is it your best time? Figure out what subtly sucks away time.
- Resource Check. Walk around your home and places where life happens. What evidence do you see of where your resources go?
- Energy check. Carefully consider where your energy is going as a parent. Where is your child's energy going? Make a list; is it the right number of directions or too many?

Table Talk

- What do you think it means to do your best?
- When do you think it really matters to be excellent?
- What would be a reason we might say no to something we are asked to do?

 YOUTHFULNESS

"Let no one despise you for your youth, but set the believers an example in speech, in conduct, in love, in faith, in purity."

1 Timothy 4:12

Waiting her turn in the hallway, an older, experienced teacher glanced up at me as I left the office. I hoped she didn't notice my puffy, rookie eyes. I mean, who cries in a job interview? As if to announce my recent college graduation, I actually choked up before the panel of three principals. They posed the question, "Can you tell us about a child who really impacted you?" Without reservation, and with her face clear in my mind's eye, I shared how a small girl left a big imprint on my life as a student teacher. Putting her trials and her tenderness into words brought tears into mine. One of the administrators even cried with me. It made for a memorable first job interview.

And I got the job.

Acting our age is not a problem. In fact, God's careful, paced design for human development allows us the creative space to fully embrace the age we are when we are in that age. God created us to grow appropriately within every stage.

We could say, "Let no one despise you for your age." Despising means to think little of, a response likely to surface when someone isn't acting their age and stage. When toddlers climb and cling, they're acting their age. When young boys hit their silly stage, they're acting their age. When girls reach an emotional period, they're acting their age. When high schoolers experiment with independence and making their own decisions, they're acting their age. The One who made us made us to act our age.

The challenge for us and for our students lies in acting our age in an exemplary way, so someone could follow our pattern.

- In our language and conversation
- In our manner of living
- In our love towards others
- In our convictions and beliefs
- In our clean quality of life

At every age and stage, if Jesus leads the life, the life should follow the Leader.

Every generation faces its hurdles and makes its mark. Generation Alpha (born 2010-2025) includes many students today who are raised by the millennial generation (born 1980-1994). Forbes reports that just six in ten millennials were parented by two partners. In their own parenting, then, the grown up millennials typically prioritize their parenting and marriage over their work and wealth. Parenting tends to be a bigger piece of what shapes their identity. A student in generation Alpha is more likely to be an only child who receives a lot of connection and attention. Forbes goes on to say, "it appears that never before has there been such a passionate, intense and borderline obsessive relationship between two generations as the one between millennials and generation Alpha." This generation is expected to reach nearly two billion once they have all been born. I wonder what they will be known for from the lives they lead.

God calls every generation to act their age. As children learn and move through the growth process of learning and schooling, they may fully embrace the stage they're in. The fullness of their youth, whether age six or sixteen, finds expression in their speech, conduct, love, faith, and purity. Together, the displays of each developmental stage present an example to be looked down on or looked up to.

Just as sure as children will be children, so should grown ups be grown ups. Problems arise when we reach an age of expectation without reaching the accompanying level of growth. When a student in middle school still cops the attitude of a preschooler, it's a problem. If a teenager exercises the discernment of a ten year old, there's likely to be conflict. If an adult parents with the habits of an immature youth, damage occurs. By modeling the full embrace of our stage of life in the mature expression of our words and our way of life, we usher our children through their own gradual growth within each stage as it's meant to be.

Belching at the table has the power to bring a group of six year olds to tears. Whispering in cliques has the power to bring a sixteen year old to tears. Retelling the story of a small girl with a big heart has the power to bring a principal to tears. God uses all of it, every lesson in every stage of life, to craft an example of a life lived with Jesus as the leader.

Digging Deeper

4 Ways to Act our Age

- Learn about the developmental stage your student is in, so you know what is reasonable.
- Scrub out the phrase, "Act your age" from your parenting talk.
- As you pray for your student, thank God for the stage they're in, asking Him to help you appreciate and enjoy it. When you hit hard stages, prayerfully ask for extra grace to see their growth from God's perspective.
- Prayerfully ask God to show you if there are areas in your life where childishness needs to be replaced with a mature example.

Table Talk

- What do you think a younger person might see in you and want to copy?
- In your age group, what kind of behavior would you look down on?
- Do you know someone just a little older than you are who is a good example? What makes you think they're a good example?
- What friend helps you to act your age in the best way? Mom, share about a friend you have who helps you too.

Carter, Christine Michel. "The Complete Guide to Generation Alpha, The Children of Millennials." Forbes, Forbes Media LLC, 21 Dec. 2016, forbes. com, Accessed 26 May 2019.

ZEAL

"Do not be slothful in zeal, be fervent in spirit, serve the Lord."

Romans 12:11

It's never been easier for a child to be lazy. Today's toddler is tempted to turn from curiosity and fall into the black hole of a hand held screen, numbing interest and excitement before they take hold. At the same time, a lack of passion and productivity collide in what Western culture sees as a major problem, one unfamiliar to grandparents and parents who had paper routes and walked to school. Laziness grates against our love of meaningful labor, and we loathe the likeness in its place, but it's hard for grown ups to take action too. Are students today doomed to life lost in video games and virtual relationships?

No one uses "slothful" as a compliment. Conveying an image of a backward, sluggish person, we work to rub slothfulness out of our student like jelly on a cheek at church. Make no effort, and it's likely our amazing human child will slide down the slope where sluggards go. Sensing it would be perfectly normal to pick up speed if they merely start down that doomed path, we set timers, limit screen time, insist on homework first, and take away tech in attempts to help young ones learn laziness leads to loss and initiative is the better way towards independence.

Each child looks at their lazy self in the mirror and decides to stay lazy or break free.

With intensity, moms and dads waffle between pleas for a response and gasps of disbelief at their child's ability to appear lifeless. Only the sound of a text notification has the power to awaken the lost from distant slumber. Parents want the same for students that Romans 12:11 wants: a zealous child with a strong spirit.

Zeal comes from the same word describing boiling water. A hot heart loves what is good or bad in a fervent, strong way. This love points in the direction

71

of serving God cooperatively, obediently, not falling behind in living well. Fully alive and engaged, when life is lived with a hot heart for God, laziness is left behind.

Every child will wander down their own lazy river, discerning between true rest and quiet or slothfulness and waste. Students need to know how the two approaches differ, learning self-regulation as part of the human need to slow down. Our good urge to rest can be distorted into a negative slump. From their earliest days, never do for your student what they can do for themselves. Allow them to learn the lesson of effort-making and enjoying the fruit.

Some children wander down the lazy river longer than others. There are real reasons why some give up. We're not talking about the occasional unmade bed or last minute assignment. Excessive isolation has the potential to set a child up for despair, stealing away hope or willingness to participate with others. Distractions at every turn in our noisy world threaten to take a child's interests hostage and hide them from true activity. Comparison painted in pictures telling stories of other people suggest there's no use trying to join life, because the standards are unattainable. If a child stays too long on the lazy river, whirlpools of despair, distraction and comparison may be the cause of entrapment.

If your student needs to break free, resist the urge to name your child by their challenge: "You're just lazy!" Heavy words around the neck of a growing child have the power to pull them down the slothful slope even faster. Instead, identify the behavior and outcomes with it: "You're spending your time in a lazy way, so now you'll miss the game." By avoiding the assignment of a child to a category, we prepare them to break free. We all have moments when we choose lazy, so use those opportunities to teach students about looking at the schedule, considering how time passes, and planning for what matters most.

We all need a reason to emerge from the chains of binge watching, scrolling, time wasting, and ignoring hot heart living. Most motivations fail eventually, and we learn to want more meaningful reasons to get up and off the couch, put down the device, or walk out the door. In the end, the only reason worth living with a hot heart is Jesus. This is the greatest lesson learned on the parenthood journey and the greatest lesson learned by our students on their education journey. We leave behind the easy urge to fall back in wasted time that adds up to a wasted life. We learn, instead, to yield our potential and our productivity to the One we belong to, the Lord who is worthy of a hot heart.

For the student, a hot heart looks like patterns of listening, participating, taking responsibility, and doing it like it matters, because God Himself made you capable for learning and for life.

For the parent, a hot heart looks like creating a home where Jesus is known, being an example of serving Him, starting new each day in a fervent way, and letting go of our lazy, so we welcome the life the Lord intends.

Let's walk away from the lazy way and lead our learners in hot heart living!

Digging Deeper

3 Ways to Zeal

- For one week, make a note of how you spend every 30 minutes. What do you learn?
- Make a list of what you want to be zealous about. What gives you a hot heart?
- Ask a friend to pray for you to be fully engaged with your time.

Table Talk

- How do you feel when you let yourself be a little lazy? What about when you let lazy last a long time?
- What abilities has God given you to make good things? Art? Writing? Helping others? Listening? Counting?
- How would it look if those gifts fell backward? What if they were strong?

Acknowledgements

To the moms who have invited me to be their mentor at home and abroad, over coffee and over Skype. You and your kiddos have taught me so much in our times together.

To the many children and families of Eastern Oregon who inspired me while I wrote these ABCs, especially the Policy Council mamas who opened their hearts to me. You kept this message fresh on my heart and mind.

To Mr. Hayes who first hired me. You modeled what it is to be a compassionate educator and leader who cares about showing children the love of Christ.

To my sweet tribe of friends who love to pray and prayed me through the season when the ABCs were being written on and out of my heart. What a gift you've been to me.

For my mom who showed me Jesus and then prayed for me and still prays. Where would I be without your prayers? I'm so grateful for the commitment you and Dad had and the sacrifices made to launch me on my education journey.

How glad I am for all those who first used the ABCs and wrote to tell me how they were blessed. You were the first to teach me to see the potential. Thank you for letting me know.

Great thanks to Christen Price, visionary and friend, who saw what the ABCs could be and did what she does so well—she invited me. God knew we would walk through days of change at the same time and this project of bringing the ABCs to life would bind our own hearts together and give birth to sweet things. Your patient encouragement and confidence fueled me. I'm so grateful to have received such grace from the powerful partnership of Christen and Raleigh.

Thank you to Samantha Whittington, of the Christen Price Studio team, who made the words better with care and kindness.

To Jeff and our grown-kids who have encouraged me to use precious time to think and pray and write. I am grateful you treat these things with value and as gifts from God. How blessed I am by all I have learned at Jeff's side and for the encouragement he has given to help me teach beyond our borders. The world is our classroom, and I love teaching and learning in it with you.

He already knows, but I have to acknowledge that my Heavenly Father has been the One to use education to lead me to life. Because of Him, I know parenting and teaching are sacred callings.

About the Author

Julie Sanders is a teacher committed to encouraging grown ups to engage the power of prayer in their student's education. She isn't sure when she first learned to love learning, but education has been written in her story as long as she can remember. Over more than twenty-five years of work in education, she has been a teacher, professor, mentor, tutor, consultant, trainer, and leader. Most recently, she directed early learning programs across Eastern Oregon. Julie's professional experience and education shape her message of lifting up learners through the power of prayer.

As a communicator, storyteller, and teacher, Julie loves creating truth-filled, practical tools that speak to the needs of people. She is the author of *Expectant: 40 Devotions for New and Expectant Moms* and a regular contributor in the *Pray the Word Journal* series. She is also a contributing writer for *Chicken Soup for the Soul: The Multitasking Mom's Survival Guide*.

Julie is a sojourning Southerner, living in the Northwest with her husband Jeff of three decades. They love working together cross-culturally and helping people learn what matters most. Their own two students are now grown and off to teach around the world. It makes Julie's teaching heart happy.

Julie prayed through every day of her daughter and son's educational journeys. As a mom and educator, she loves helping others know how to pray for their students in what matters most for learning and for life.

www.juliesanders.org